stay weird

COLORING BOOK

sebastian blume

ISBN: 978-0-6480847-6-1 paperback.
BIC Subject category: 1. Drawing-coloring books for grown-ups 2. Arts & Photography- techniques
3. Craft, hobbies- art 4. Self-help-art therapy & relaxation 5. Self-help-anger management. 6.Self-help-stress relief

Stay true to you.
An original is worth
more than a copy.

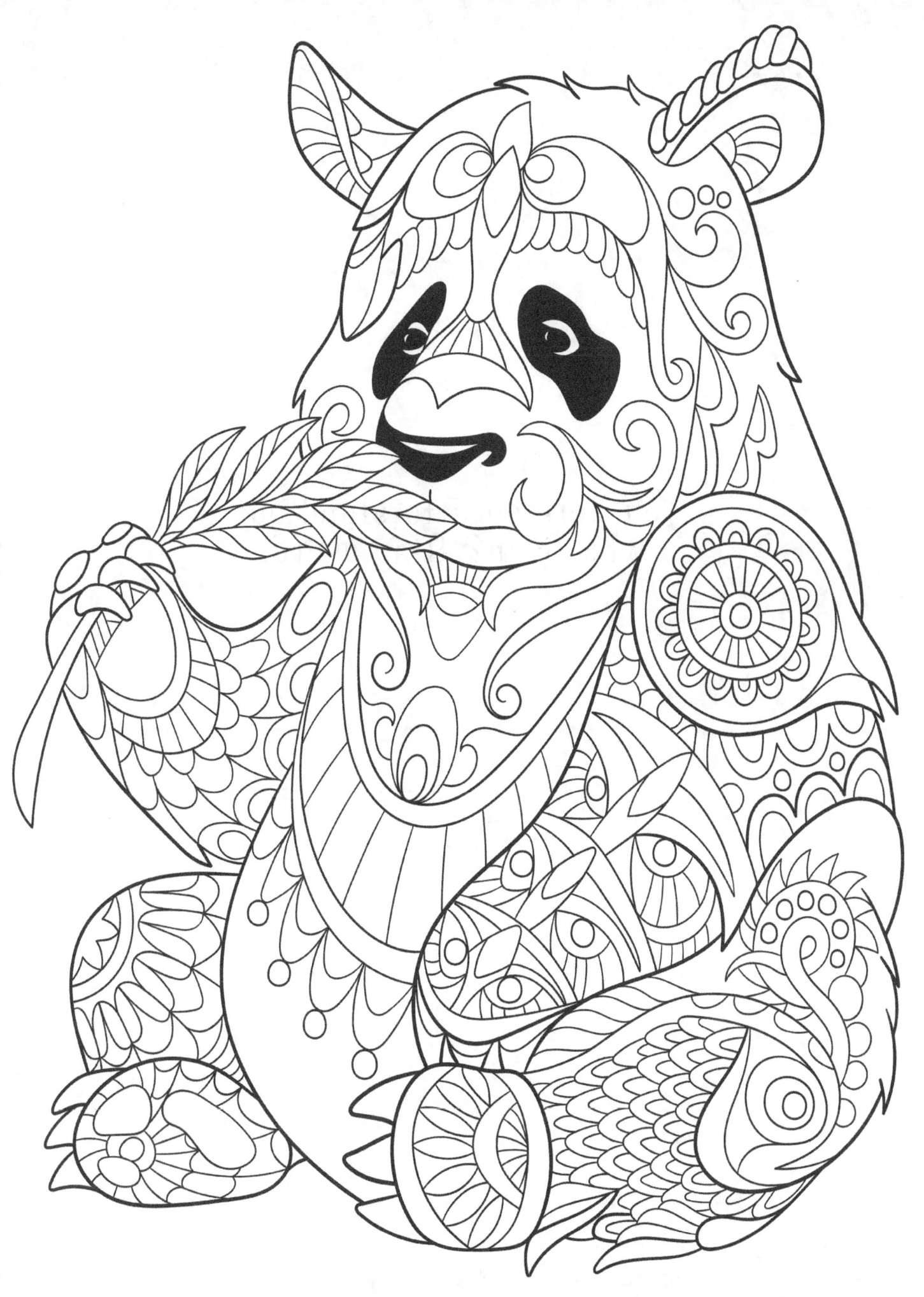

You were born to stand out.
Why fit in? Stay weird.

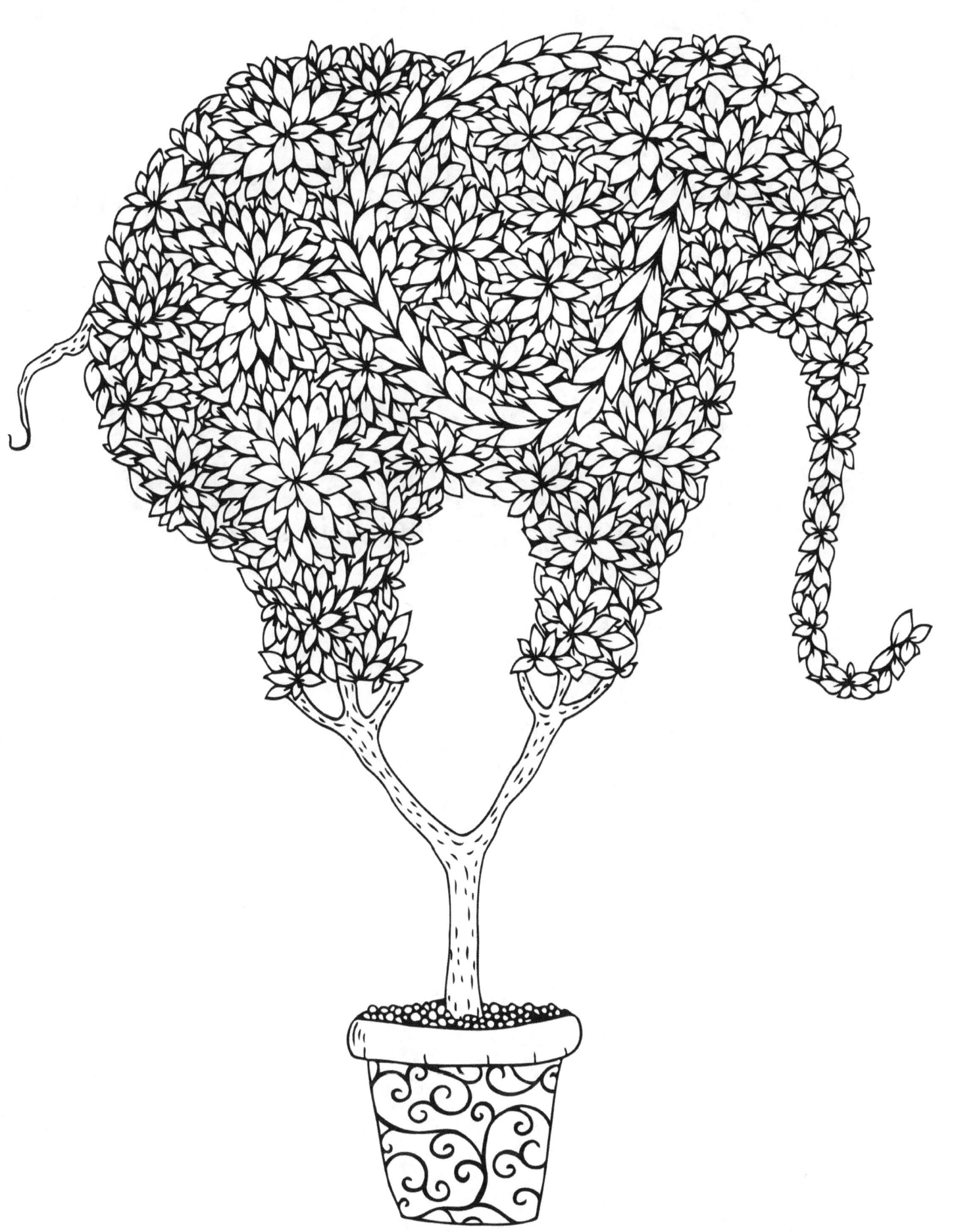

Do whatever, be weird it's ok.

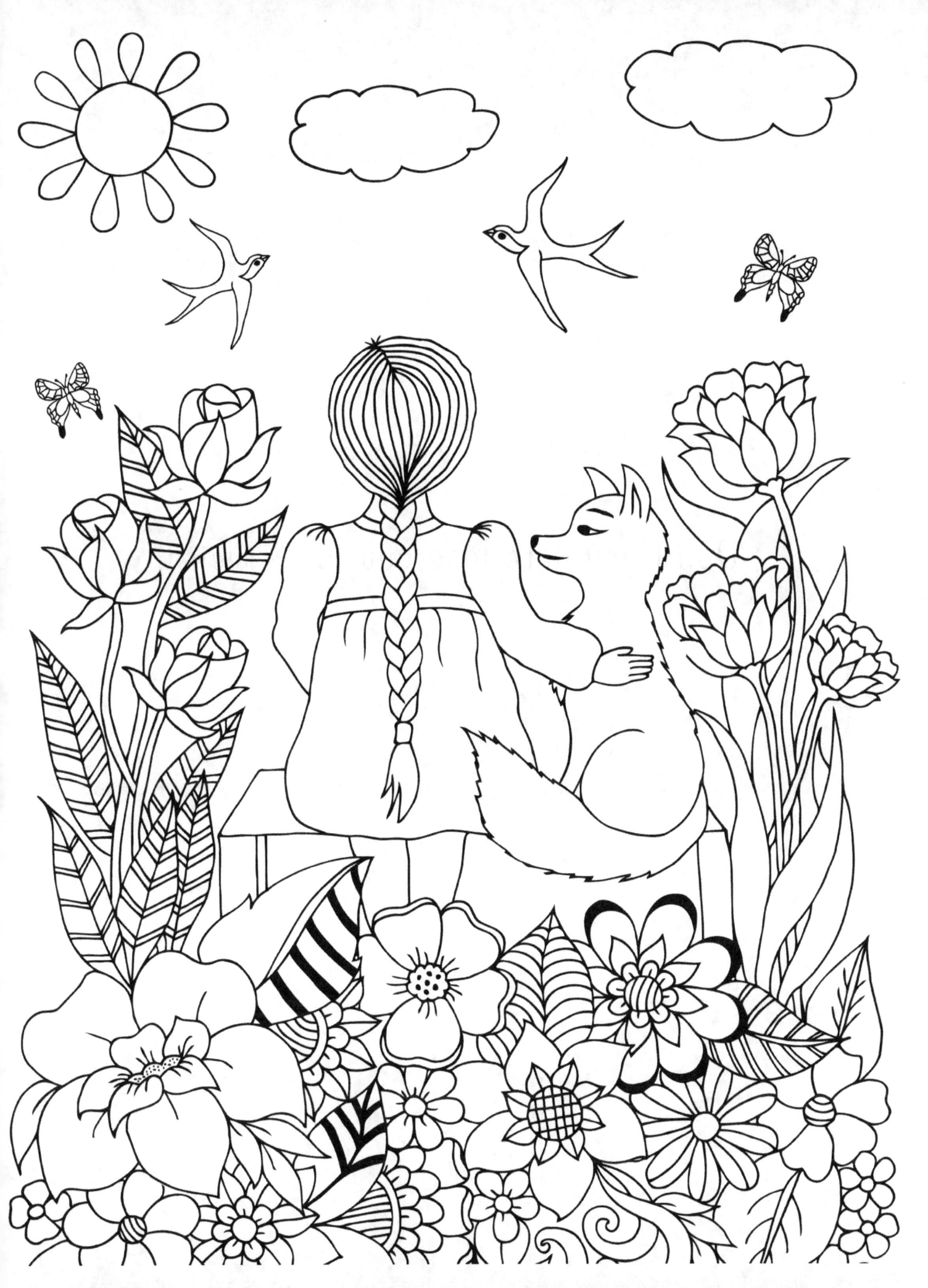

Don't you dare lose you. Stay weird.

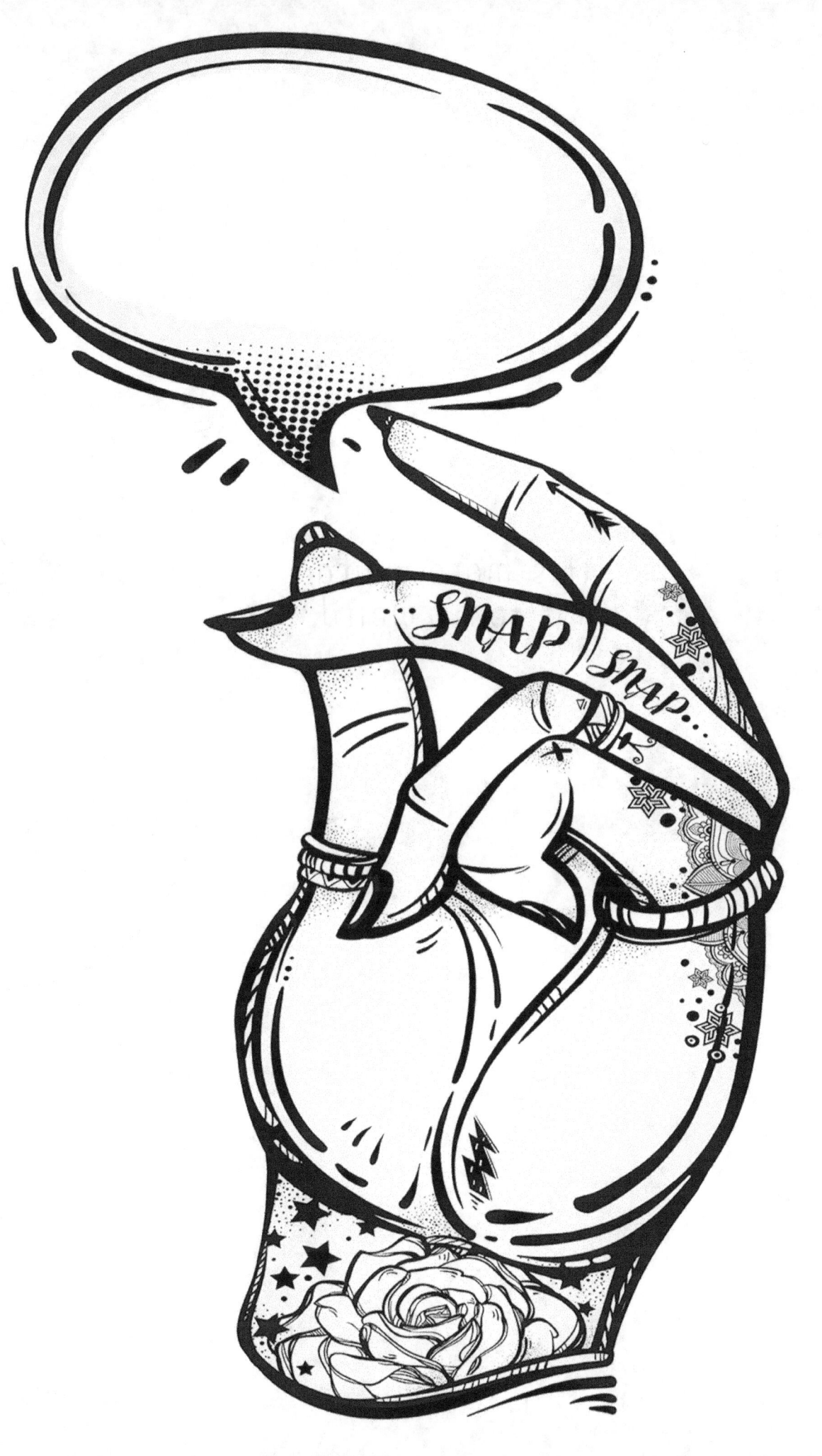

It's more weird
not to be weird.

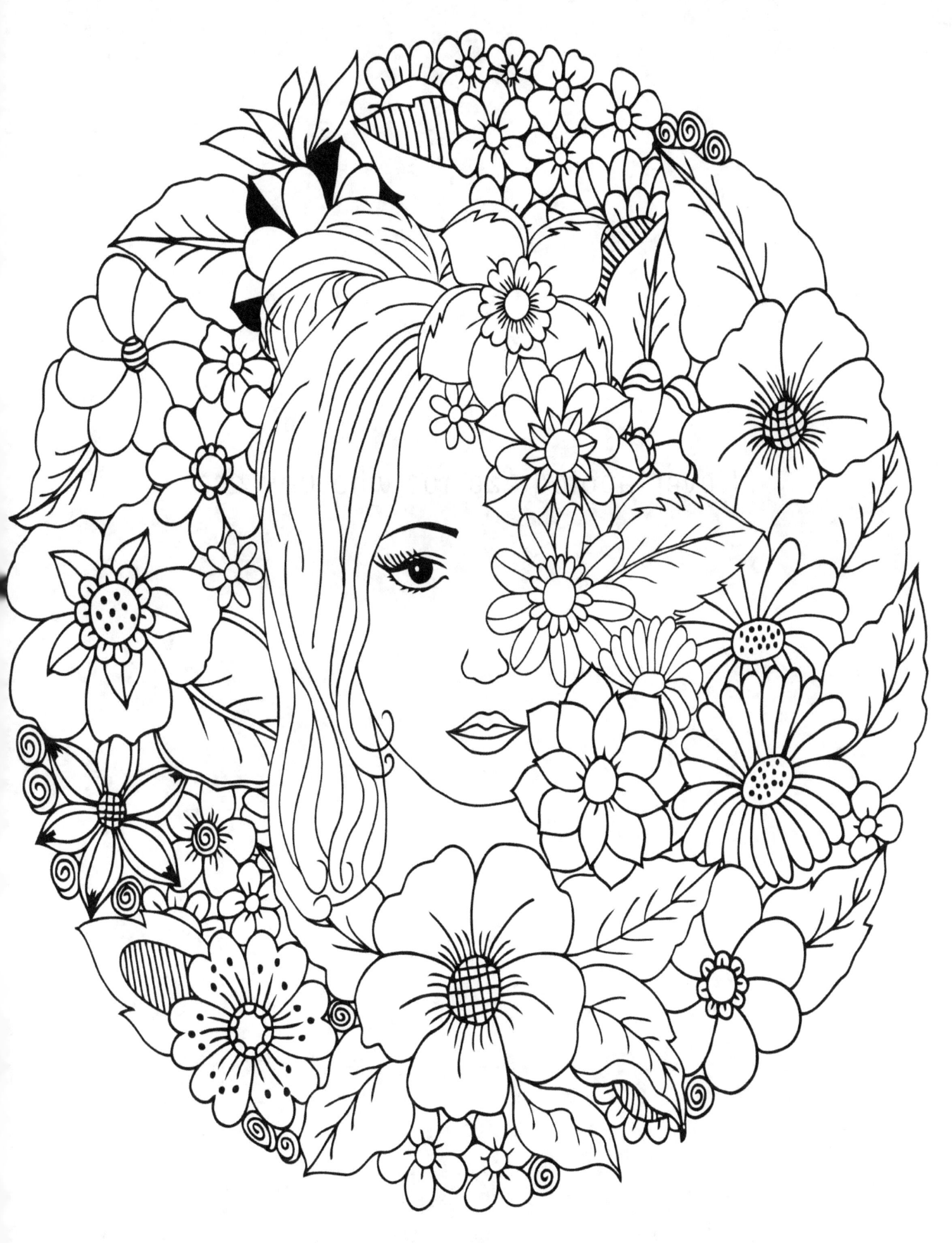

Never apologisze for who you are.

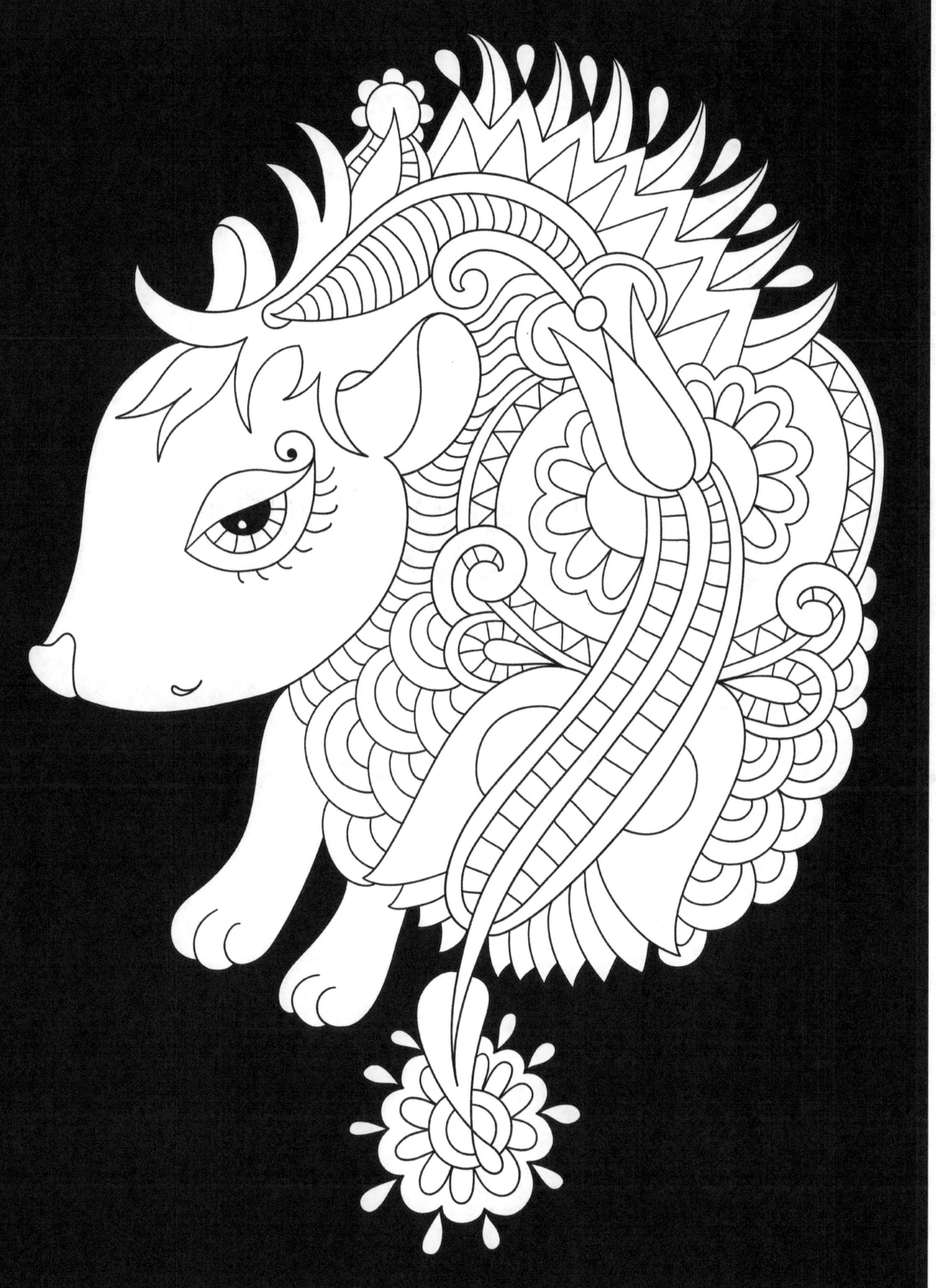

Stop saying yes to sh*t you hate.

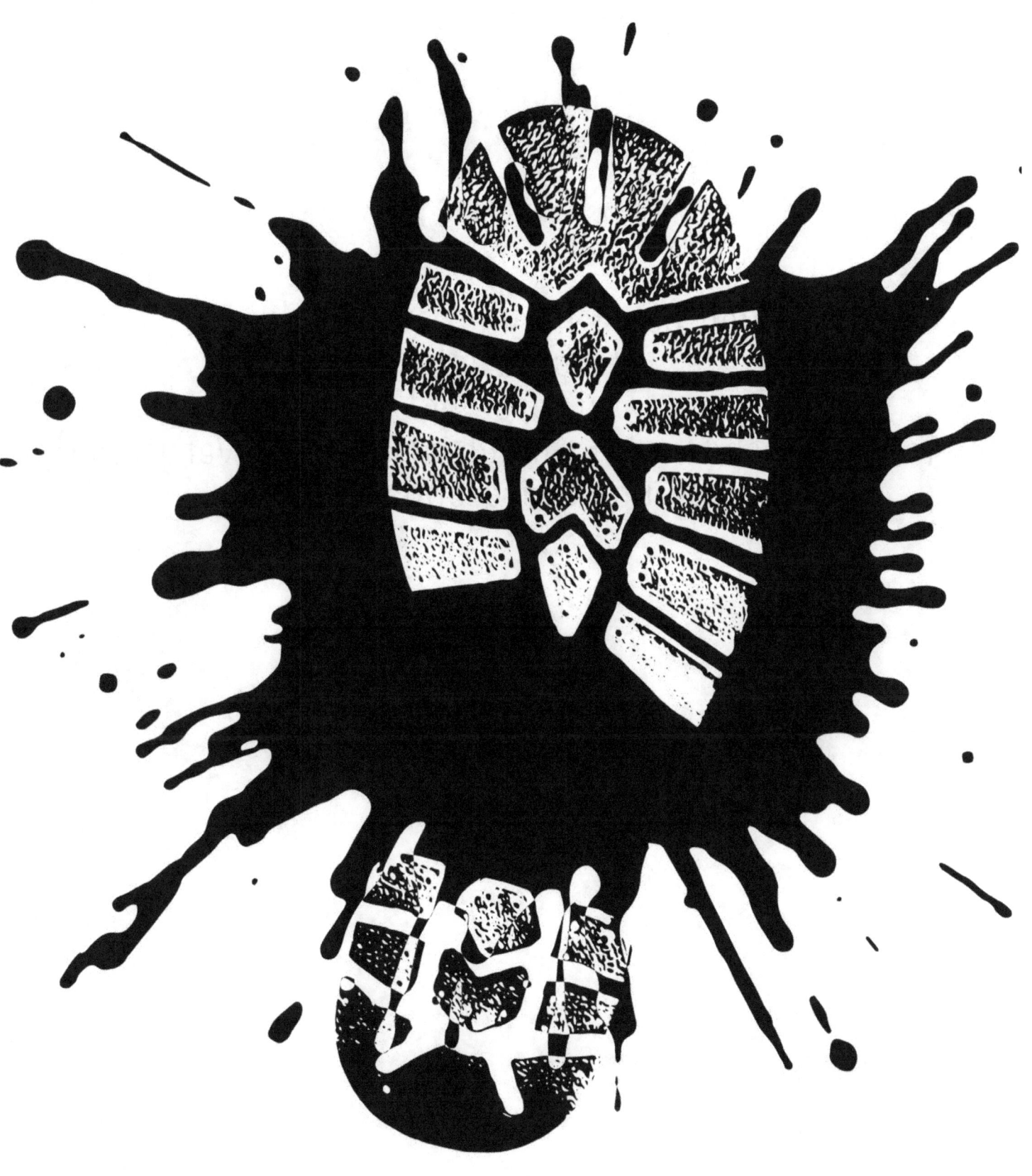

If you can't handle my weirdness,
(stupid jokes)
(sarcasm)
(and my tendency to laugh at almost everything)
you're not weird enough for me.

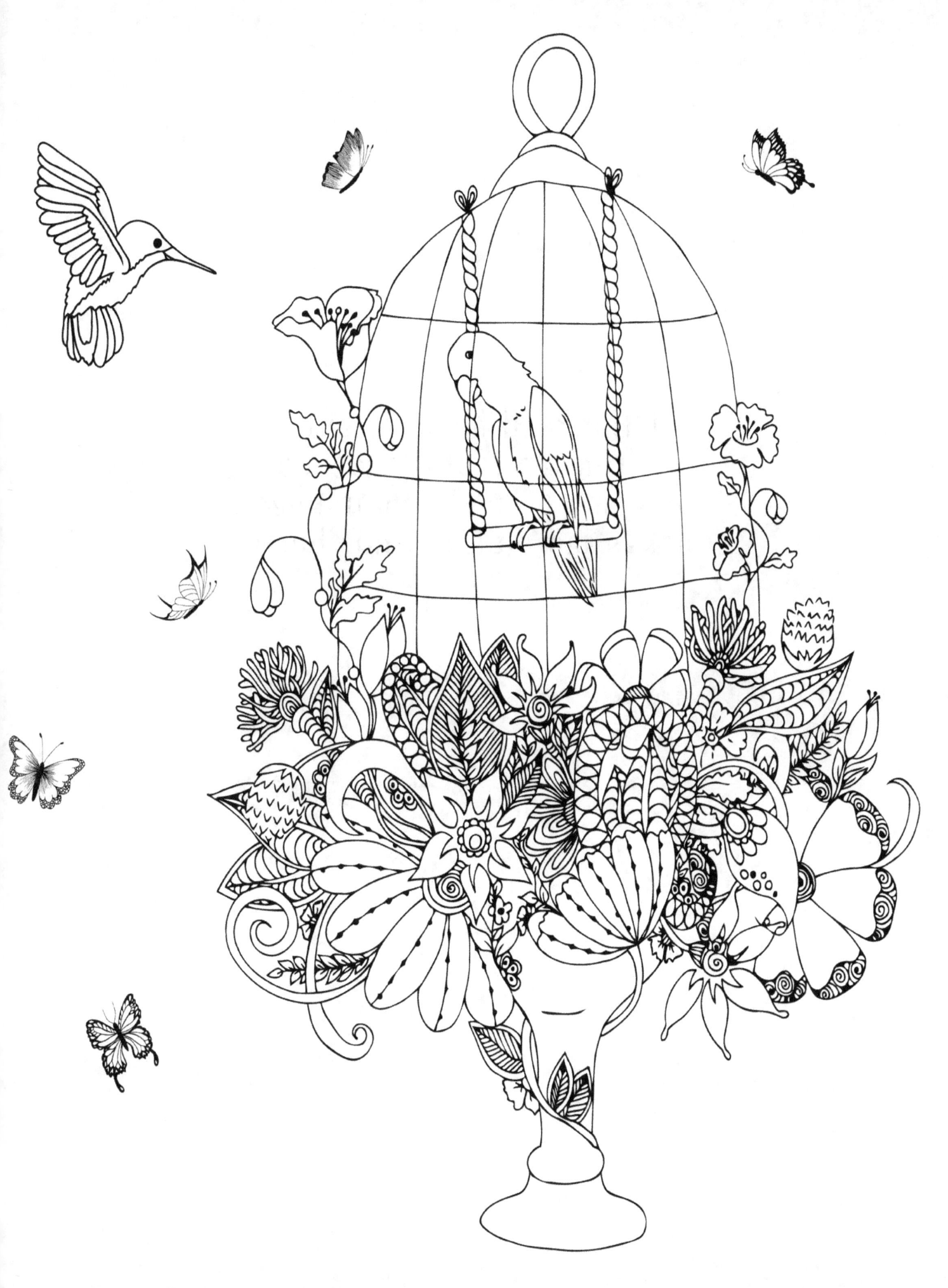

I think all humans suffer
from an identity crisis
at some point in their lives...
makes me glad I'm not human.

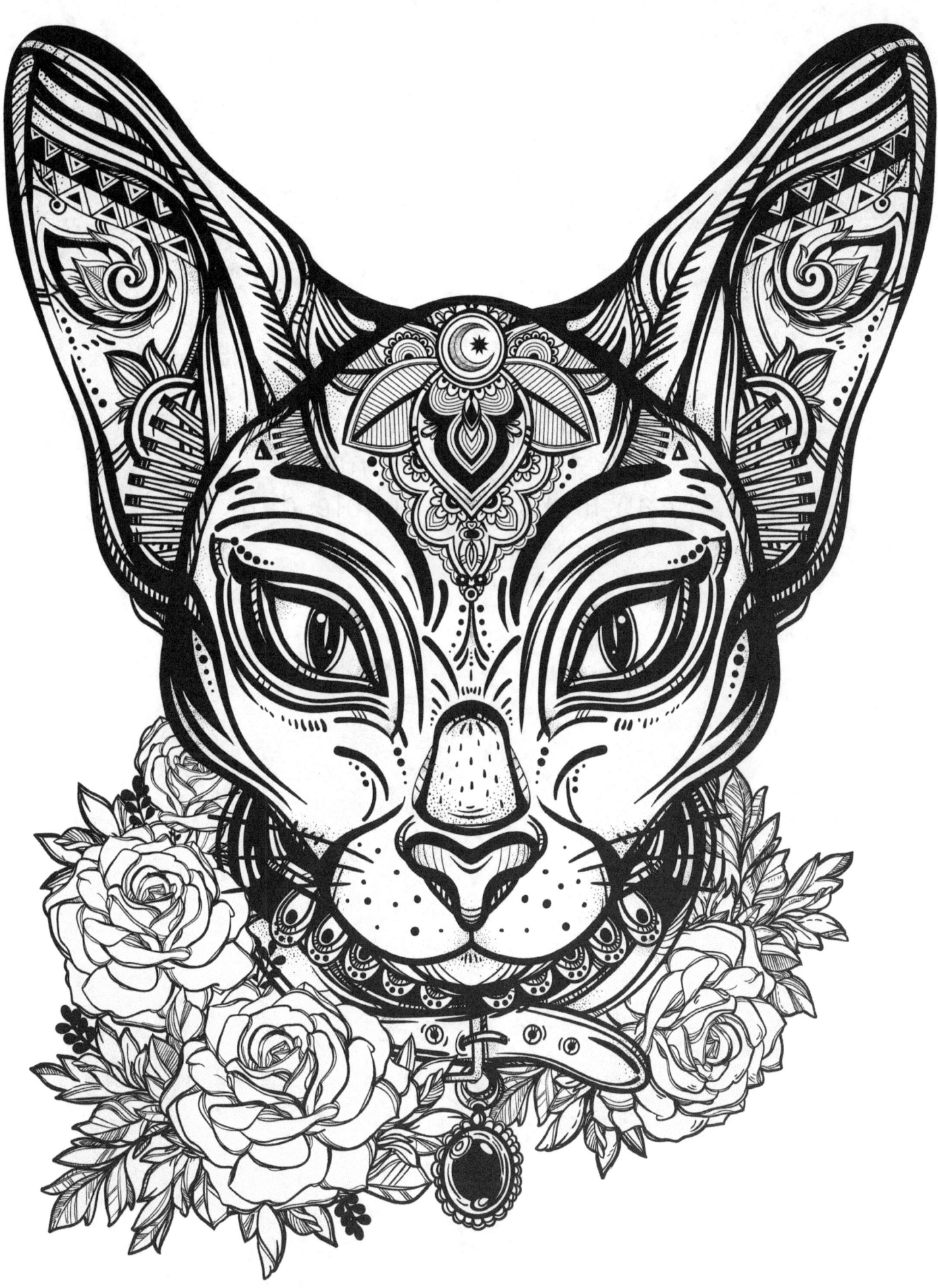

One small piece of weirdness
in the morning
can make your whole day.

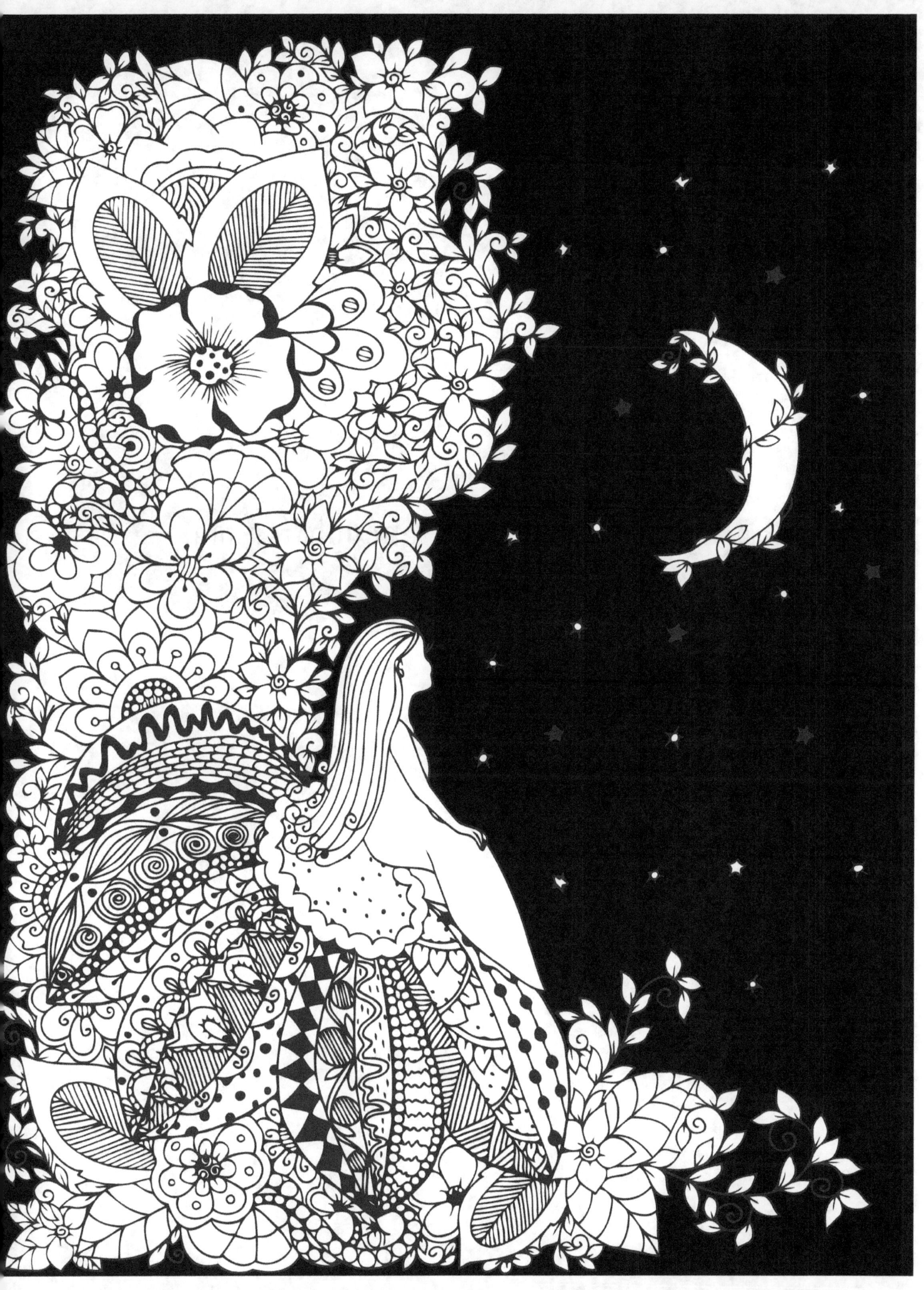

Weirdness is good enough for me.

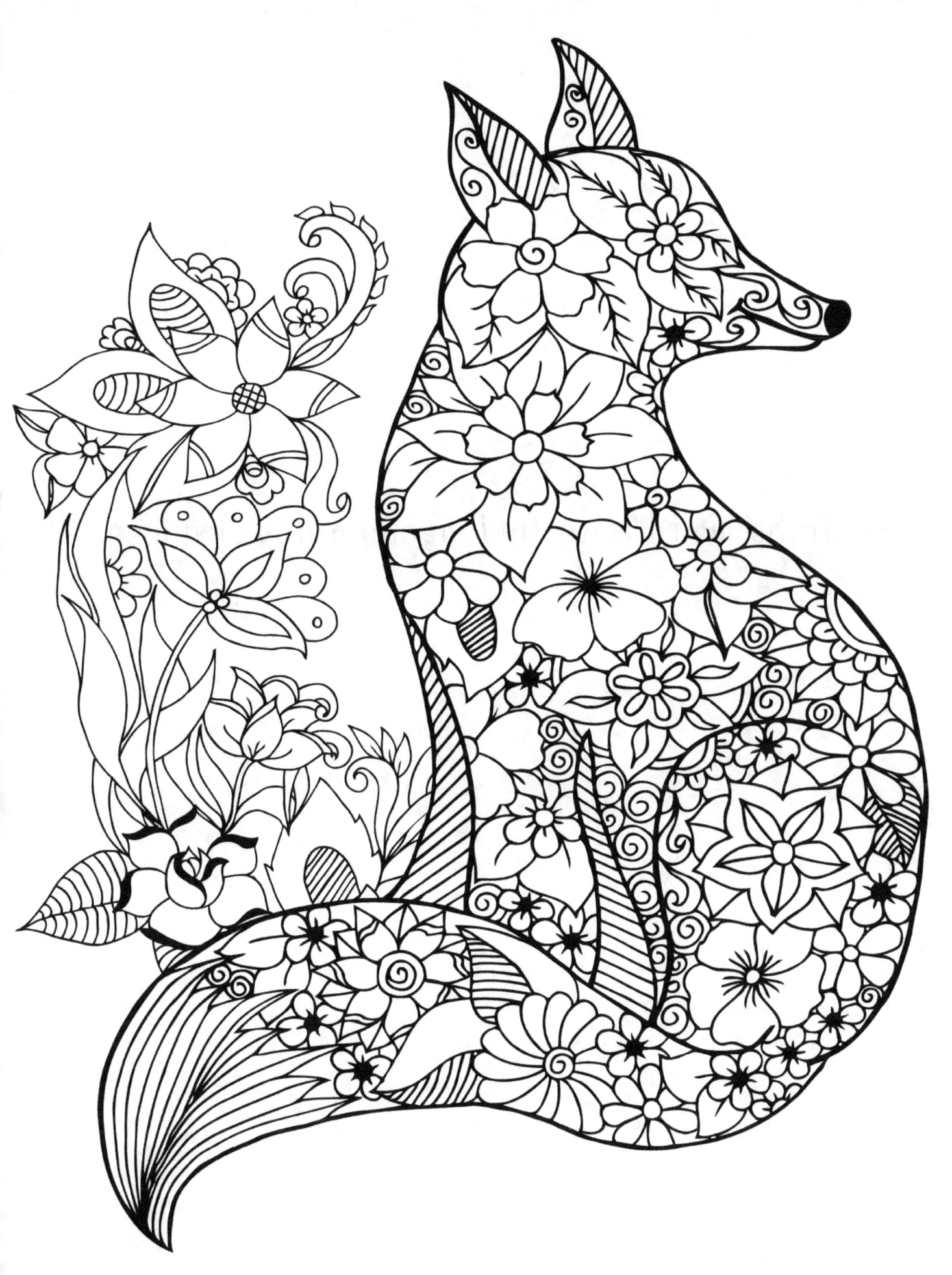

To be weird is to find meaning in weirdness.

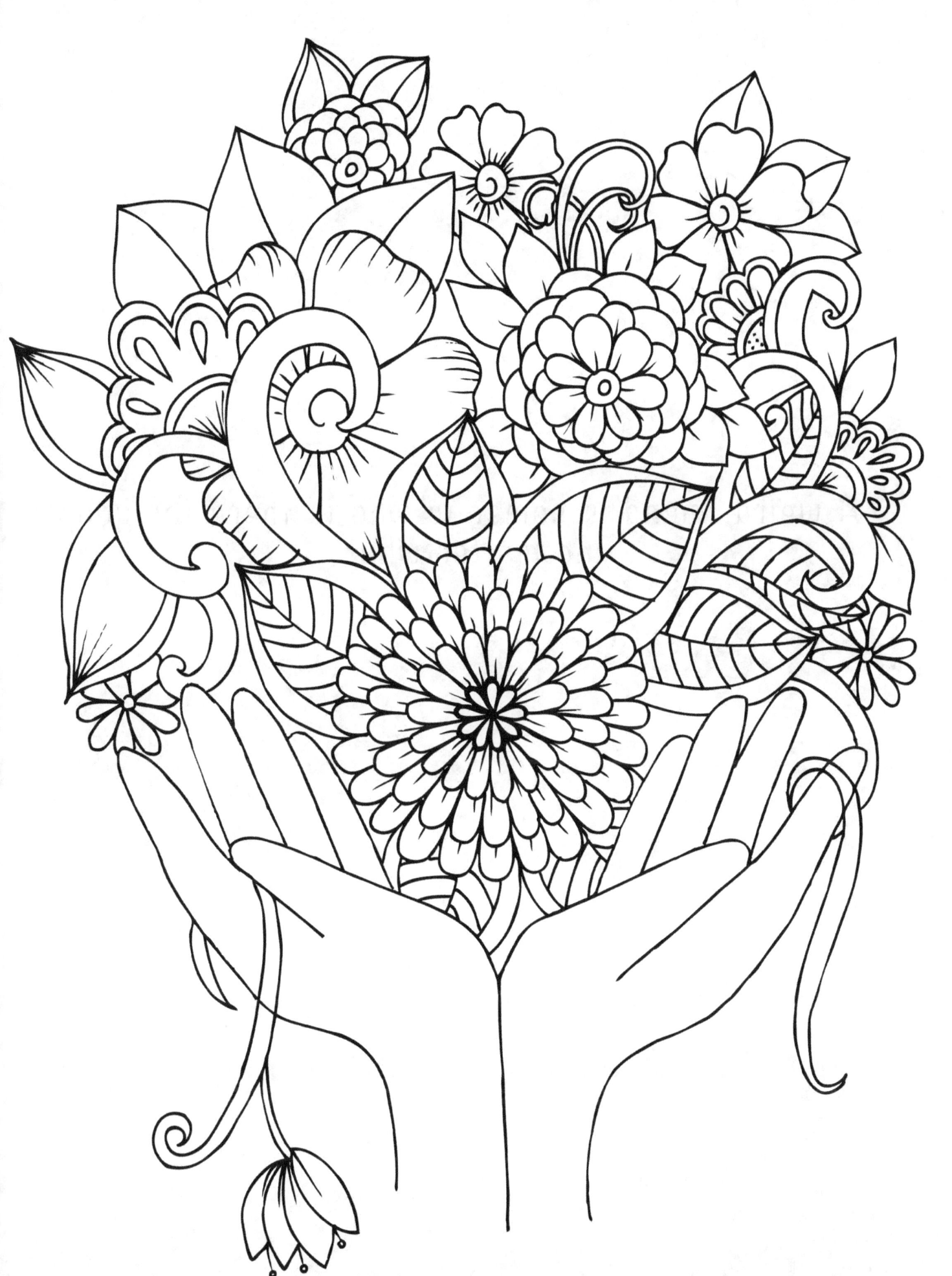

A weird friend is someone who is there for you,
no matter what.

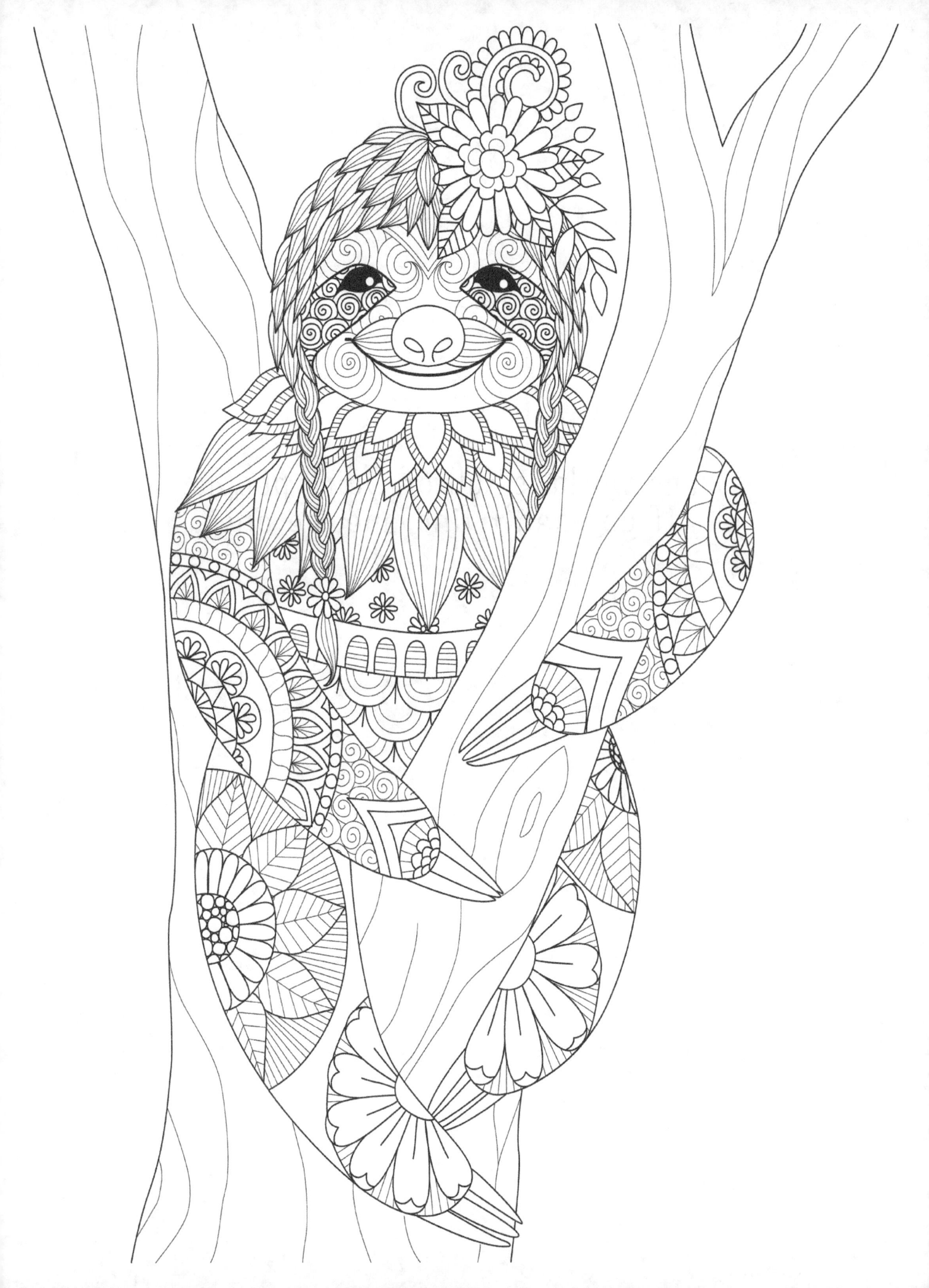

The world is full of weird people.
If you can't find one, be one.

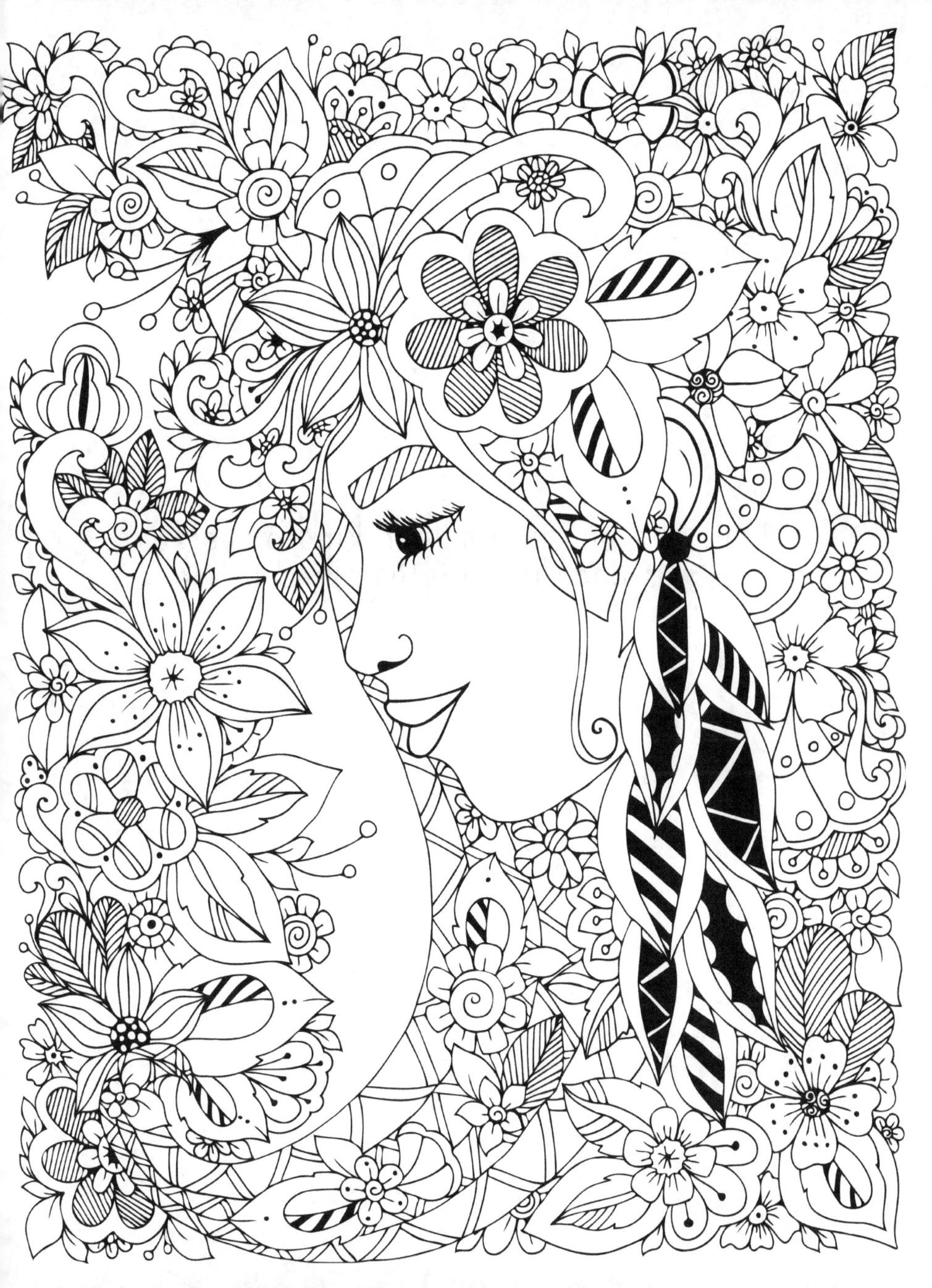

I'm not a one in a million kind of person.
I'm a once in a lifetime kind of me.

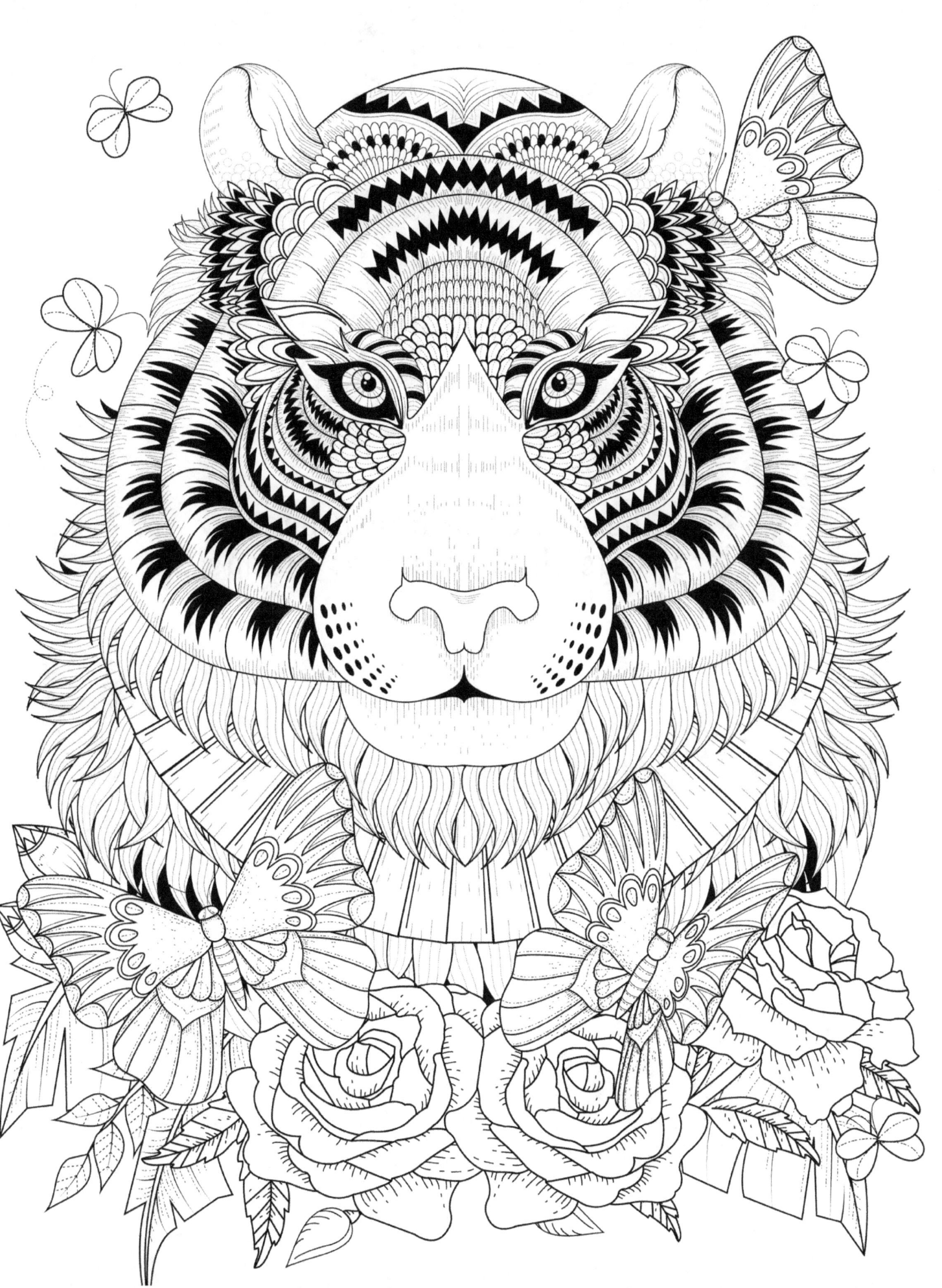

In the sea of ordinary people,
it's always the weird that stands out.

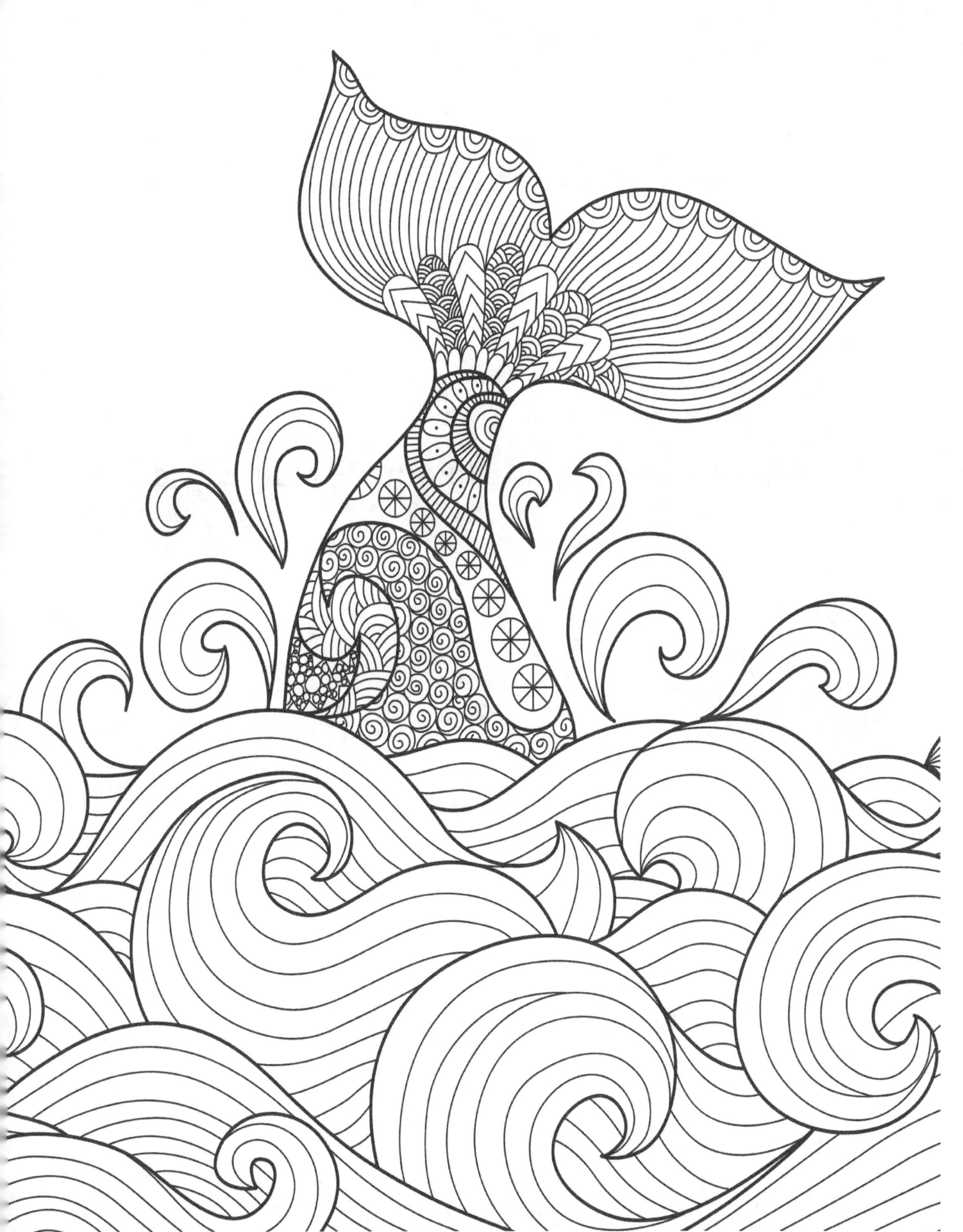

Stay true to your destiny - stay weird.

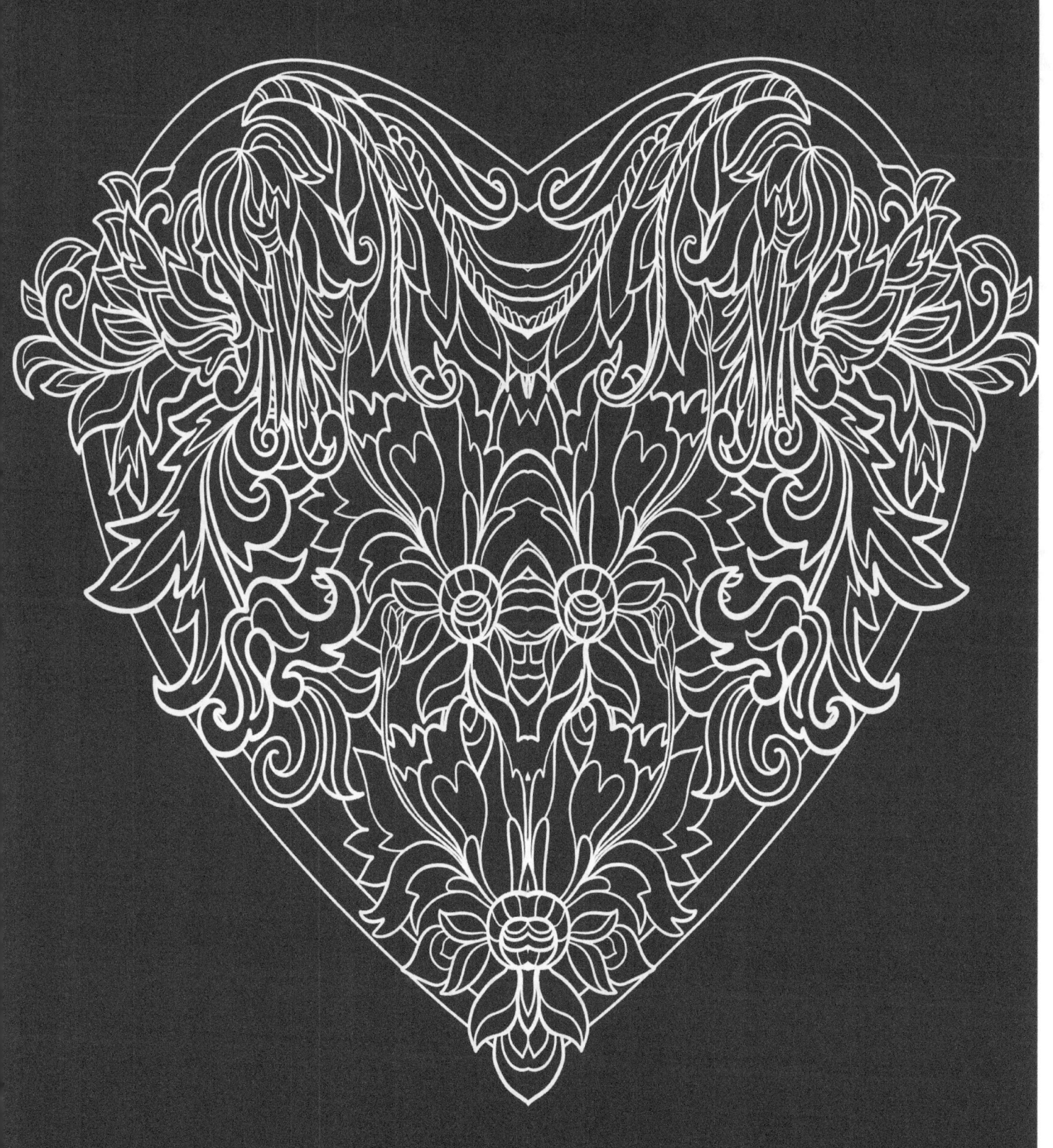

I'd rather be weird than boring.

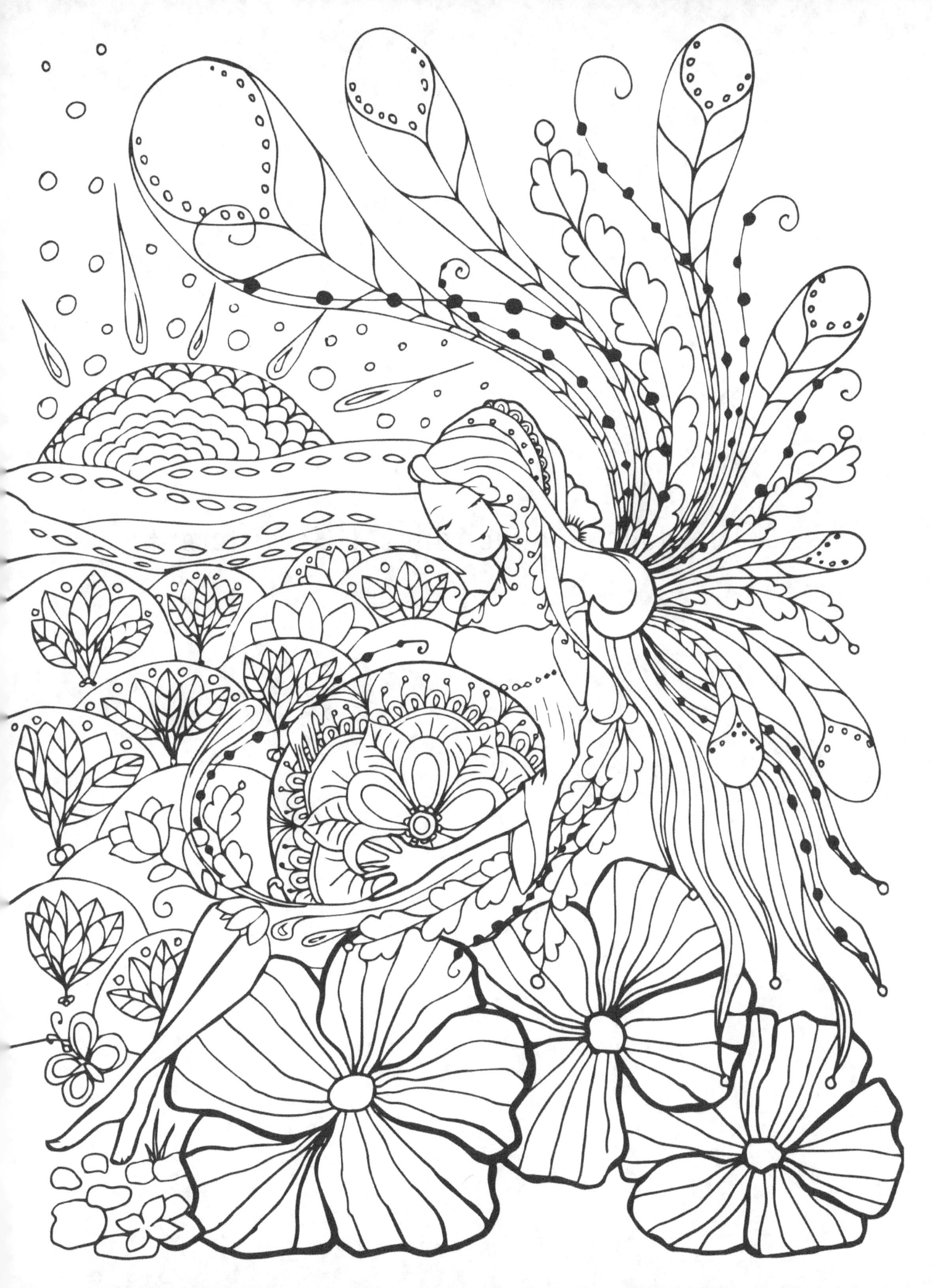

Own your own weirdness! Be different.

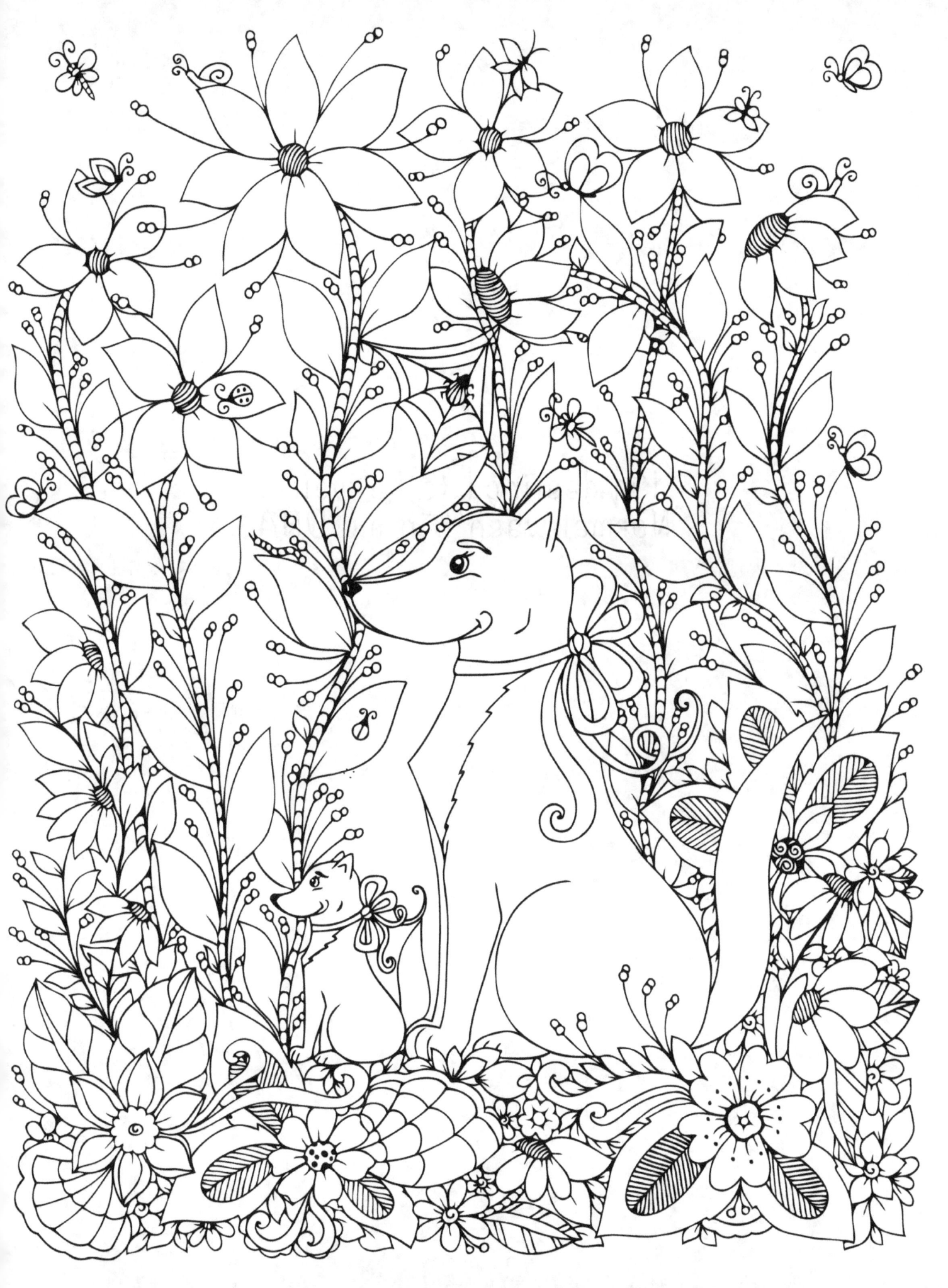

I'm destined to be weird.
Normal wasn't in my DNA.

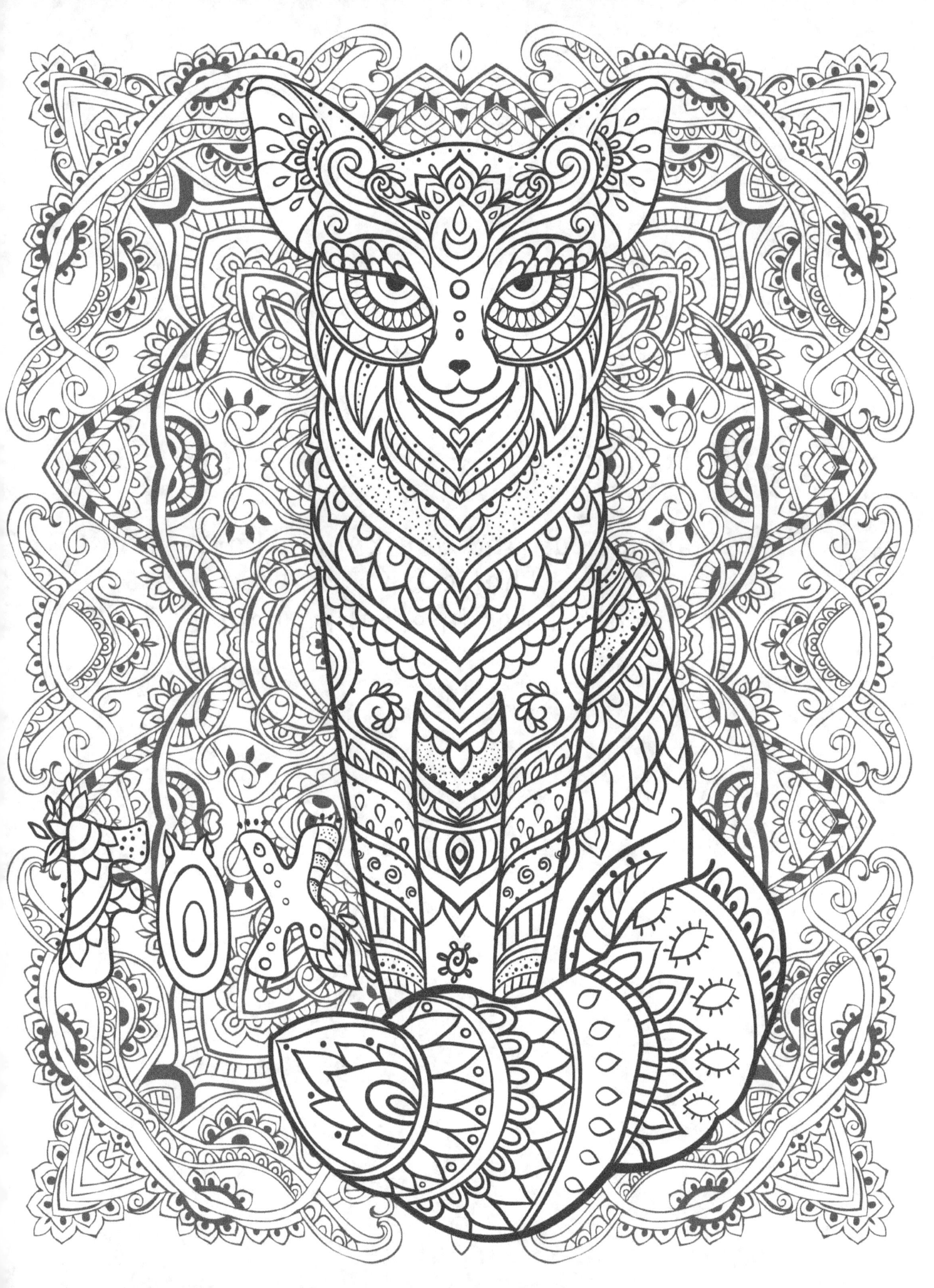

I am weird. And you know what?
That's OK.
so are the most interesting people.

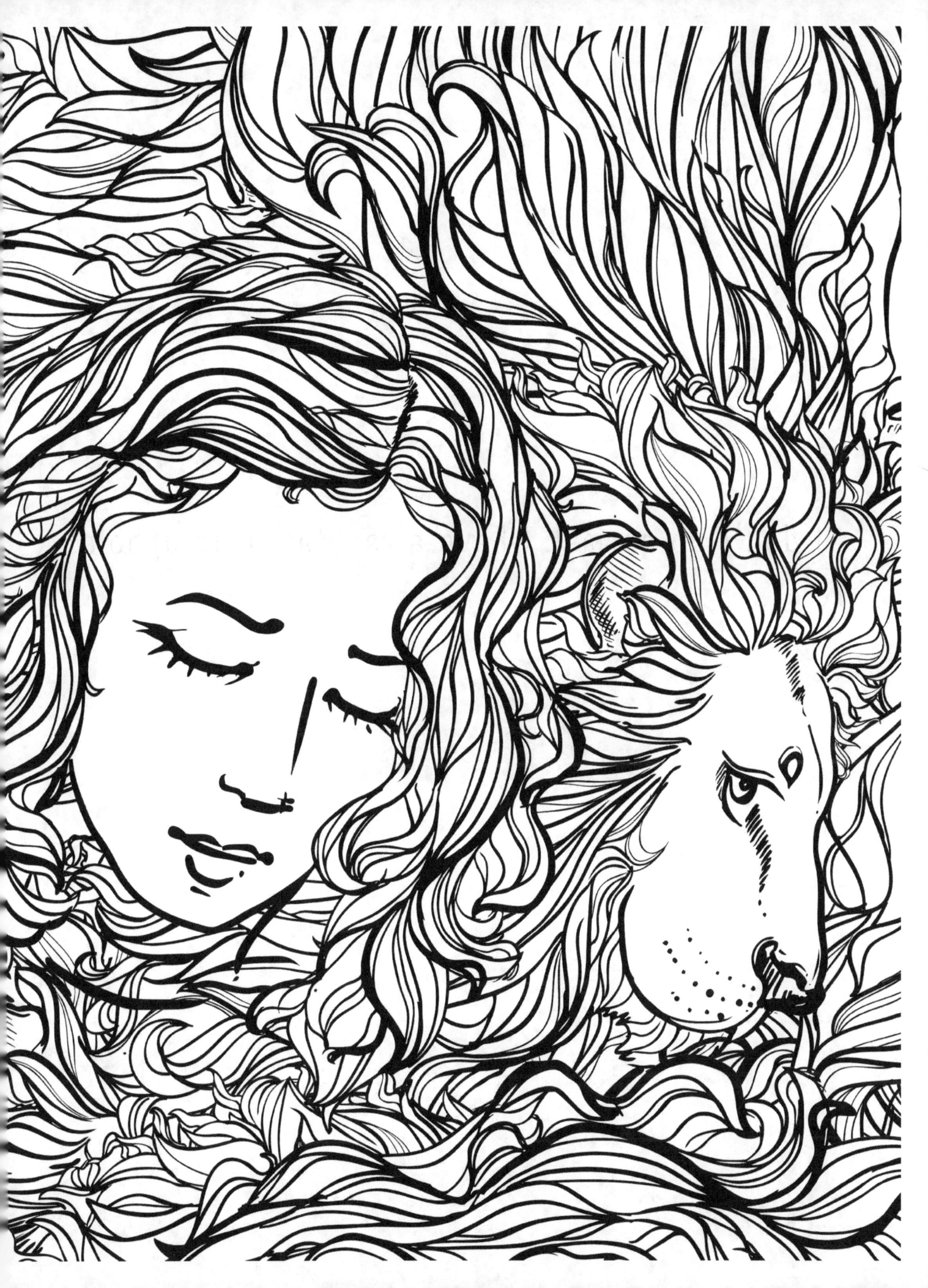

I don't do normal. I have a reputation to uphold.

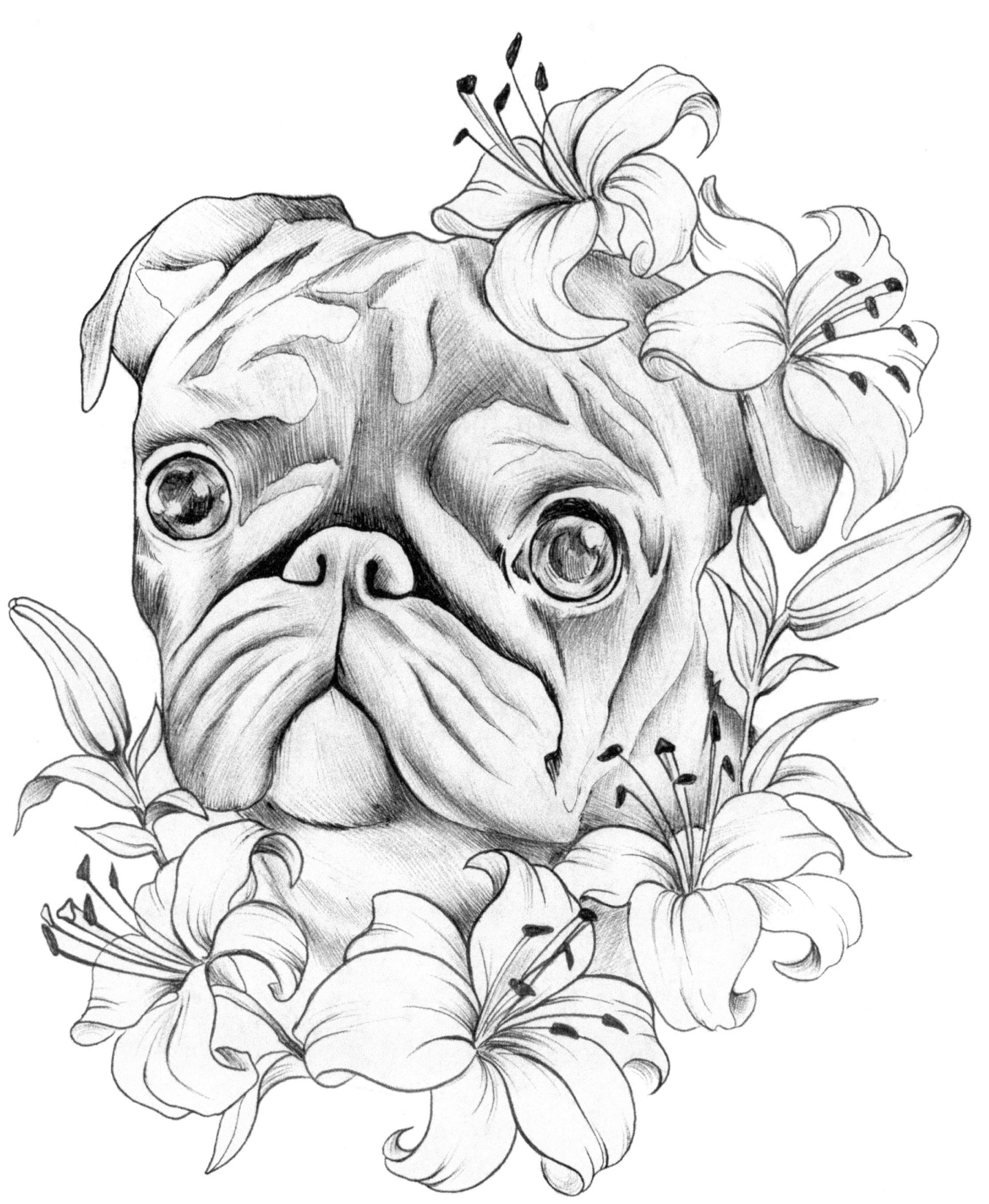

Normal is like boredom.
There is nothing sensible
you can do with it.

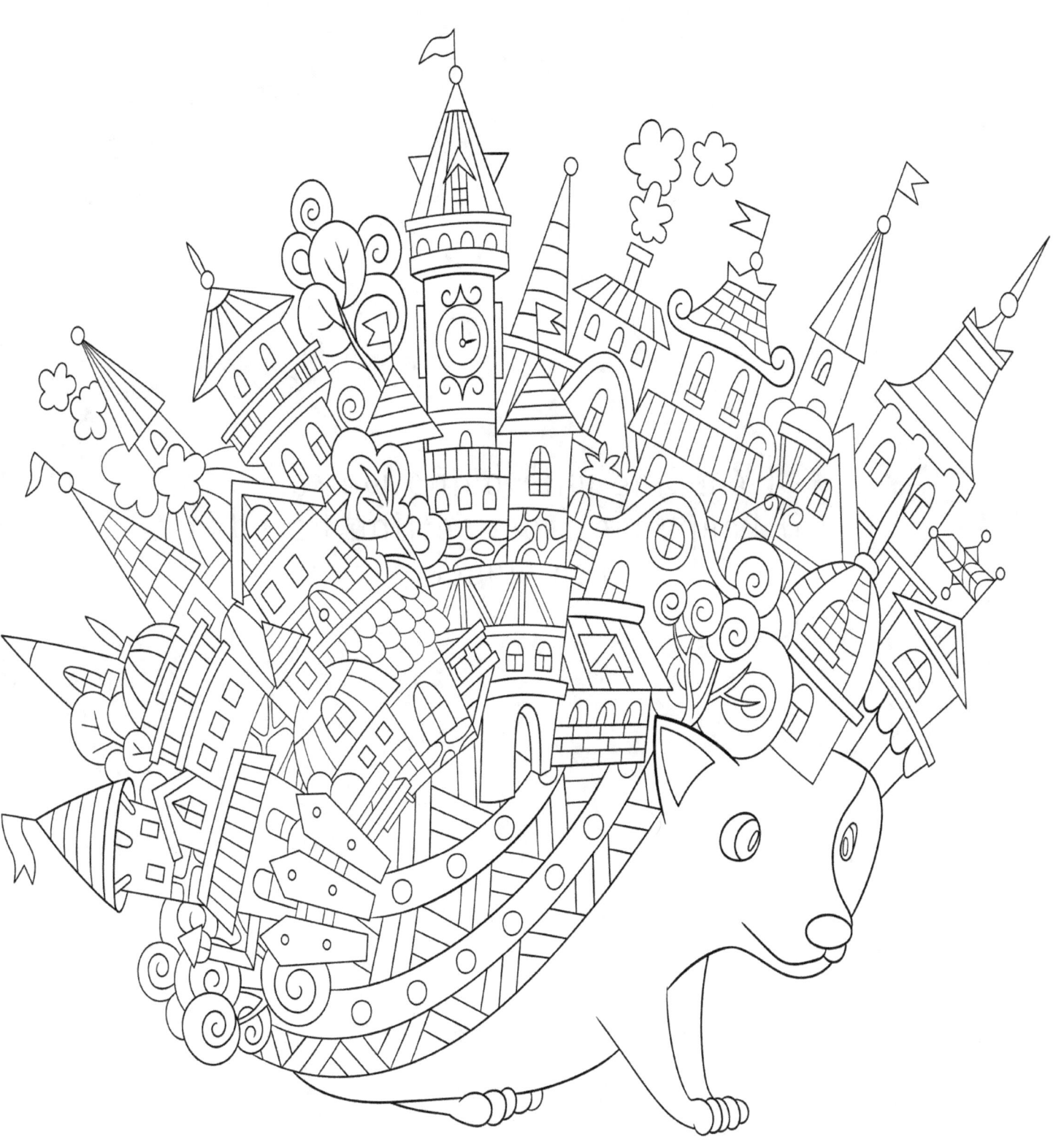

I am fine with being weird...
it keeps me from getting bored
with myself.

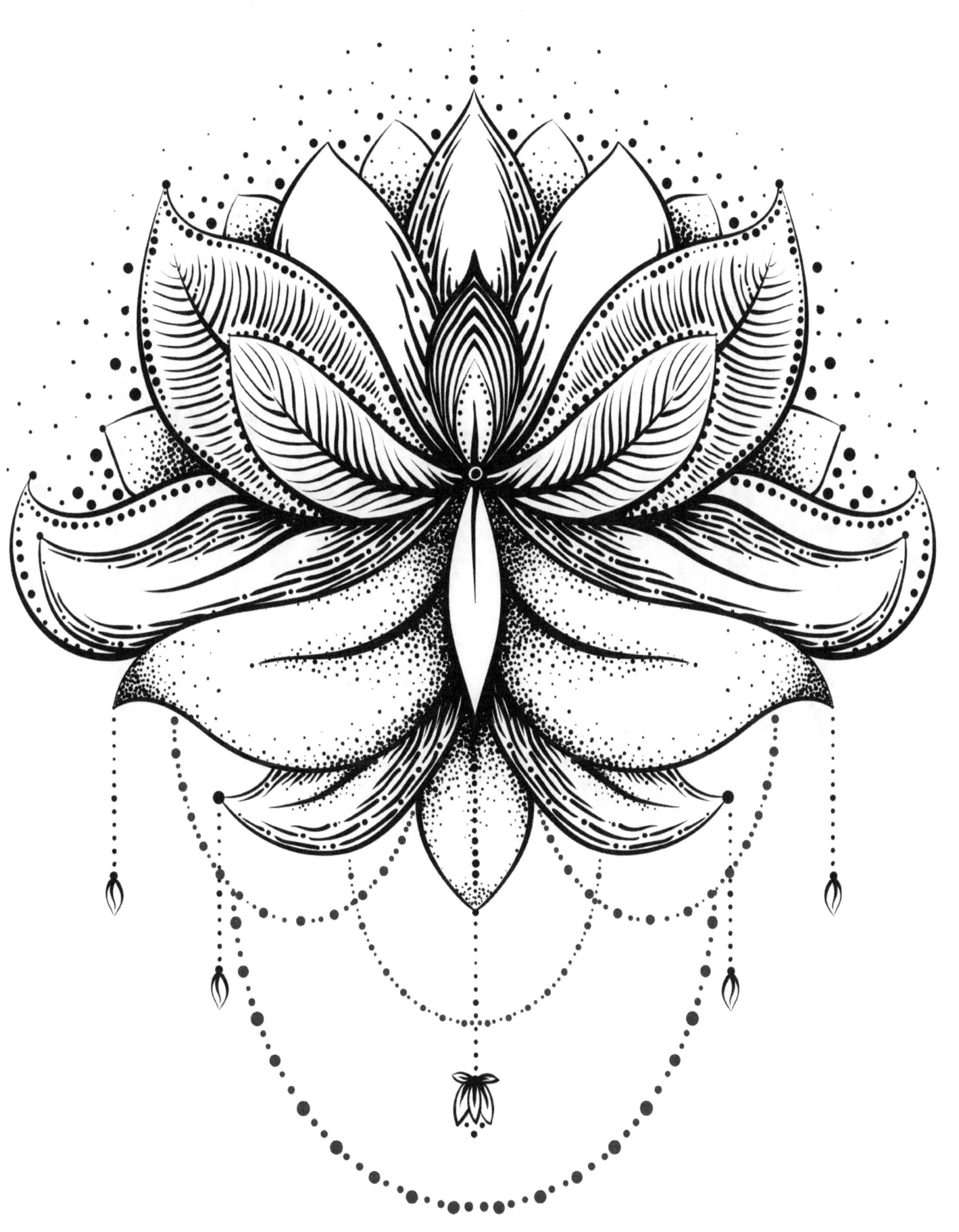